# UNRAVEL

# UNRAVEL

A Poetic Journey to You

ROWAN GHALY

ISBN: 979-8-9865833-0-3
Library of Congress Control Number: 2022912910

Illustrations: Anna Markovets
Cover Art: Rose van Der Ende
Chapter title definitions from Merriam-Webster (Inner Workings, Imagine, Create, Return) and Collins English Dictionary (Surrender) with pronunciation by Oxford (Surrender)

Printed in the United States of America.

www.writtenbyrow.com

*in loving memory of my darling grandma—*
*my lighthouse and favorite memory.*

*for the ones finding their way*

# contents

# inner workings

*plural noun*
*: the parts (of something) that are only known*
*by the people who work on it*

*love is the binding force*
*that weaves all things together.*

*unravel*

unbecoming
everything you are not
means becoming
all that you are.

rewrite the stories
you were once told

come undone
unravel
unfold
until all that remains
is you.

*author*

today you write it
tomorrow you read it—
the book of your life.

live the story
you hope to read in the end.

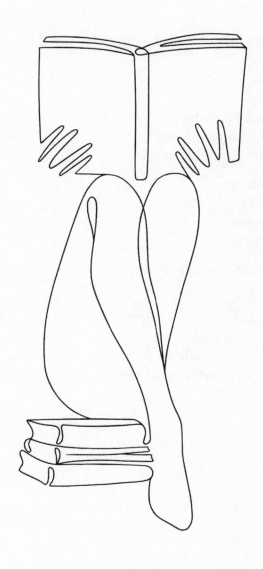

i am still learning
not to let these phases
faze me—

the hiding
the seeking
the finding
the healing.

some days i want to disappear

other days
i embrace
my celestial roots
and like the moon
light up the entire night sky.

*rebirth*

like the seasons
we wither
endure
weather
and come alive again

the transient nature of life
demands that all things
evolve

the journey is yours to define

the odds are yours to defy

*dear inner child,*


i did not celebrate you enough growing up.
i did not know how to see you, be you.

i return to you now with deep knowing
and with kinder eyes
as your loving friend.

i celebrate our oneness
as we journey together.

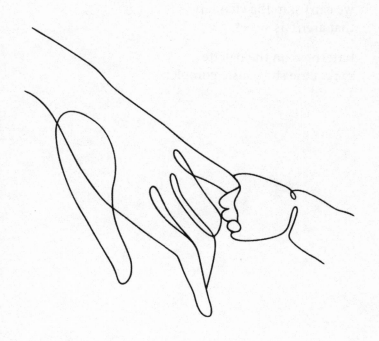

*chapters*

we can't skip the chapters
that aren't as sweet.

bitterness on the palette
makes the story taste complete.

*passing through*

storms visit us all in the same way
that we are visitors in this world.
neither we nor the storms
are meant to stay forever.

*nostalgia*

no matter how far in life we roam
love always has its way
of guiding us back home

and she
is a vibrant vessel
carrying her ancestors' dreams

she's careful not to shatter
her people are never forgotten
because of the bridge she continues to be

*the stories keep us alive*

*immigrant*

no matter where she was
home for her
always seemed far

with roots and wings
she ventured off
to build a home within

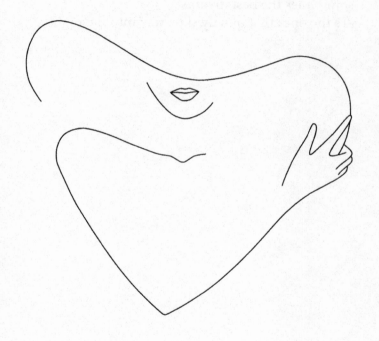

*forgotten*

sometimes the best dreams
are the ones that quietly slip away into the night

*bound*


bits and pieces
of places and people
make up who we are today

miscellaneous memories
gently pressing
leaving inked internal impressions
that bind us together

*touch*

silent
yet they speak volumes
so i read between the lines

your hands are a blueprint
i foresaw the plot twist
by searching the index

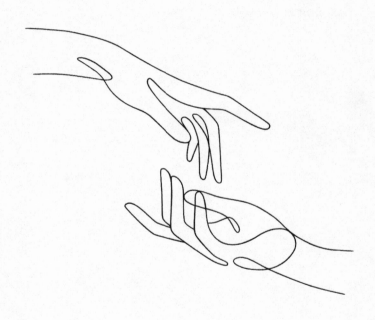

knowing when and how
to water the plant
is how the garden thrives

*the plant is you*

*alchemy*

the feelings you dread the most
are the ones that turn into gold—

sadness into strength
loneliness into love
pain into peace
and emptiness into ease

*allow the transformation to unfold*

*the light is you*

your courage and curiosity
will open the doors.
your smile and sensitivity
will take you far.
your warmth and wisdom
will move mountains.

when life falls in love with you,
let it.

someday
today will be
a distant memory.

unfold the present
and marvel
in its "ordinary" moments.

*on presence*

whether it's the beginning of a new chapter,
the end, or somewhere in the middle—
enjoy where you are now.
you'll never be here again.

*bold*

the ones who taught you to hide
did not realize
that the best place to hide
is in plain sight

*poetry*

darling,
your life force
is a poetic expression
even your smile lines rhyme

*words*

just as words can comfort, strengthen, and heal,
they can also hurt, shatter, and destroy.
let the words you pour be soothing and pure—
to others and yourself.

*illusion*

even when we get what we want
there's always something left to fix
it's a constant game
of trying to attain
perfection that doesn't exist

*reflection*

how we see others depends entirely on how we see
ourselves. we cannot expect change from others if
we are unwilling to change ourselves.
transformation begins within.

*fragile memories*

mirrors shatter
but reflections remain
a consciousness contained
in the fragments of our stories

your fantasy
is a pending reality
a subconscious dream waiting
for you to conjure and create it

*what are you holding onto*
*that needs to be released?*
*set yourself free.*

# imagine

imag·ine | \ i-ˈma-jən

*verb*
*: to form a mental image or concept of*
*(something not present)*

*imagination creates all possibilities.*
*love opens all doors.*

*imagine growth*

be patient with your growth process.
the fruit trees
may take seasons to cultivate
but the nectar and shade
are worth the wait.

*imagine thriving*

trust the ebbs and flows of life's seasons.
ask for support when you need it.
you deserve to thrive.

*imagine connection*

connect with your soul
connect with your source
connect with the world.

it's all an energetic exchange.

*imagine abundance*

there is space for you
and it is safe for you
to shine.

allow yourself to.

*imagine adventure*

step boldly into the unknown.
your fears are here
to free you.

*imagine joy*

trace the roots of your happiness
and plant more seeds there.

*imagine purpose*

you cannot rush divine timing.
what is meant for you
will arrive right on time.

the growth
the thriving
the connection
the abundance
the adventure
the purpose
the joy

—all of it
is already yours.

*imagine that*

*let your creative power lead the way.*
*where can your imagination take you?*

# create

cre·ate | \ krē-ˈāt

*verb*
: *to bring into existence*

*speak beautiful things into existence.*

*manifest*

if you believe it will happen, it likely will.
thoughts are powerful seeds.
water them with faith
that good things are coming your way
and watch the garden begin to grow.

*work of heart*

doing the heart work
is the hard work.

dive in
rediscover your inner world,
allow compassion
to course through your veins
as you navigate.

*work of art*

embrace
the intricate and infinite layers
that make you a work in progress
and a work of art

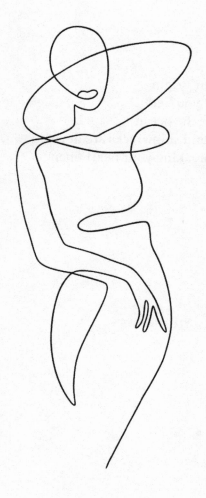

*voyage*

love is your origin
it brought you here
and love is the ocean
its waves and shipwrecks are devoted
to softly breaking your heart open

*wander in all the ways*
*that bring you closer to your truth.*

*healing*

healing comes in many forms.
some years it's a pending prayer.
some seasons it's renewed hope.
some days it's a change of heart.
and sometimes it's the storm.

*perspective*

every challenge
is a chance
to solve
to evolve
to try again.

*grounded*

some days you'll stumble
other days you'll fly
be daring and humble
on both occasions

*alignment*

release everything
that is not aligned
with your highest purpose

*on creating*

create with all your heart
and trust the creative process.

remember that not every piece
needs to be a masterpiece.

breathe
flow
find your vision.
find your voice.

begin somewhere
begin anywhere

pause if you need to
walk away if you need to
but do return.
and imperfectly create.

*are you chasing happiness*
*or are you creating it?*

# surrender

sur·ren·der | /səˈrendər/

*verb*
: *to give in (to)*

*surrender to the flow of life.*
*may peace flow through everything you do.*

*celebrate*

and so we learned to celebrate the journey,
all of it—the ups, downs, and everything in between.
the mess was just as important in the story
as was the glory.
*maybe even more.*

*dedication*

your story is written differently
no one can see through your unique lens
keep your heart open
unfold your mystery
show the world the magic you see

*artistry*

when a song gets stuck in your head,
you sing it.
when a dream gets stuck in your heart,
embody it.

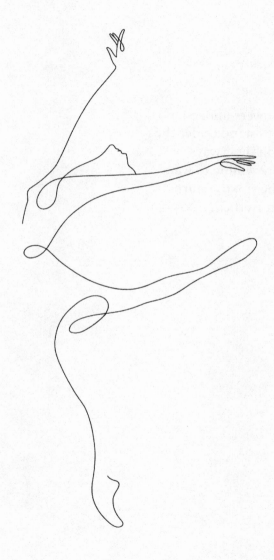

*composure*

sunflowers understand
how to stand under the rain
wise in their ways
they're willing to wait
for the sun to return
and turn them into gold

*inner treasures*

never underestimate the power of your strengths,
struggles, and passions, to come together and make
a difference in the world. it's all connected.

*on purpose*

your purpose is less about you and more about the
gifts you're meant to give the world. purpose means
tapping into your talents and using your strengths
to strengthen others.

*meditation*

sit with yourself in silence
and see what comes up.
then send it all away
and see what stays.

between hardship and healing—
there is hope.

*wandering*


even the stars and the moon
are lost
and on their way home too

while you are alive
may you be just that—
*a live expression*
of your eternal essence

*layers*

deep feeling leads to deep healing.
be willing to experience discomfort
to grow. be willing to peel back
the colorful layers and uncover
your shades of purpose.

*intuition*

the more you resist her,
the harder you make it for her
to guide you.

your intuition
will show you the way
if you listen.

*well-being*

reclaim your wholeness.
openly receive all that nourishes you.
willingly replace what drains you
with what lights you up.
gently release what's no longer serving you.

*tend to your spirit.*
*how is your heart today?*

# return

re·turn | \ ri-ˈtərn

*verb*
: *to go back or come back again*

*full circle*
*return to you*

where you thought you were heading
was never a place
but a space within
the journey of life
is a winding road
leading back to you

today i found myself
on a speeding train
life is moving too fast
with no time to hesitate
i'm forced to concentrate
on four words that cast my fate:

*focus on your priorities*

*in gratitude*

thank your body
for generously hosting you
in its only home.

thank your mind
for guiding you through
the valleys of its vision.

thank your spirit
for the worldly ride
it's taking you on.

thank your heart
for beating
and leading you home.

to return, we must first depart.
go on, there's an adventure ahead
and it's filled with new parts of you
that you still haven't met.

it's not the answers
we're after
*it's the questions*
we're in love with.

lifetimes spent
searching for more,
the undiscovered
transcends
and sends
a soul where it needs to go.

*wayfarer*

no matter the junction
you arrive at in life
you have every reason to celebrate
how far you've come
and who you've become

sometimes all it takes is
*a little bit of chaos*
to awaken
the extraordinary within

*to all of the women we once were,*
the expired and evolved versions of us
thank you for weaving us into
the women we are today

*to all of the women we are yet to become,*
this walk is one to remember
don't wait up
we're taking our time
*on this journey home to you*

rest assured
we will all meet
soon

*forward*

notice the signs
feel the gentle nudges inside
telling you it's time
to step into your next chapter

*fabric*

slip into the rare silk
made from your genuine essence
adorned with pearls of wisdom
slip into your ethereal presence
express it
liberate it
anything else is fabricated

*how has your journey shaped you?*
*celebrate that today.*

*A note from the author*

Thank you so much for reading with an open heart.

I wrote this book on my self-discovery journey, as I was searching for inner peace and the pieces of myself that had been tucked away.

Finding these words buried deep within, I wove them together to reflect on my journey and connect with you on yours.

My sincerest hope is to remind you of your inner power and encourage you to gently move through your own seasons with love and wonder.

In the same way that the illustrations slowly unravel by the end of this book, so do each of our unique journeys. May yours gracefully unfold with all you deserve and desire.

With love,
Rowan

Made in the USA
Las Vegas, NV
01 November 2022

58496515R00080